WASTE NOT
Everyday

WASTE
NOT
Everyday

ERIN RHOADS

Hardie Grant

BOOKS

INTRODUCTION

During the past eight years I have watched the zero-waste lifestyle become an increasingly popular movement. Unlike environmental initiatives like carbon taxes, which can't be measured by the everyday person, the changes we make by choosing to live a zero-waste lifestyle are easily visualised and measured. For example, it's easy and rewarding to see the results of our choices as we watch the contents of our bins and even our recycling bins decrease dramatically.

Waste Not Everyday has 365 steps to help you not only reduce what goes into your bin but to rethink how our modern-day systems can change if we learn to alter our choices. You don't need to tick off every single tip instantly or within a year. Do what you can – you might even realise you are already doing most of it. We can all make a change, and these changes don't have to be overwhelming. It's my belief that we can all try to do something to be kinder, live with more intention and take responsibility for our actions, so future generations are not left to clean up after us.

These tips come from my own zero-waste lifestyle – also called a minimal-waste or low-waste lifestyle – where my aim is to send as little to landfill as possible, both in my personal life and by calling on larger businesses to change their practices. There are knock-on effects of this lifestyle that include eating healthier food, reducing exposure to harmful chemicals, saving money, supporting your local community, slowing down your pace of life, and questioning everything you've been told is necessary. As a result, you'll feel freer and less like you have to keep up with the Joneses. I view embarking on a zero-waste lifestyle as a response to the many problems that are harming the planet's ecosystems and affecting our own health.

While *Waste Not Everyday* has tips about reusing or saying no to single-use plastics, it's about so much more. Underneath these choices is a call to reconnect to our place within the world – to pause and take a breath. It's part of a much-needed shift we as humankind need to take collectively. Our choices in the past have shaped the world but we have the ability to reshape it into a place where kindness reigns.

Where can you and I begin to be the change we want to see in the world?

My advice is to look at your rubbish. Reducing what we place into our rubbish and recycling bins has a big impact that can help fight climate change, reduce plastic, combat fast fashion and reduce pollution, among a myriad of other issues that are caused by our consumption. At the heart of all of our environmental issues is our consumption. By wasting less, we buy less and end up making less.

Join me and countless others on the journey to stand up for our environment. Let's preserve it for the future and treat everyone with kindness.

Let's start the change.

'The people who make the biggest difference are the ones who do the little things consistently.' Katrina Mayer

BEFORE WE START

Our bins hold a collection of wasted resources that are tipped into large fuel-guzzling trucks to then be buried in vast pits: a gift for the next generation to clean up.

And it's not only the contents of our bins that are wasteful. There is so much more wastefulness that happens before we end up throwing something into our bins:

- mining *new* materials to make *new* stuff
- burning coal and gas to manufacture *new* stuff and to power the lights, heating and air conditioning in the factories that make the *new* stuff
- draining rivers and lakes for manufacturing goods and growing crops like cotton
- producing stuff in countries with lax labour laws, exploiting workers who are not paid properly or whose safety is not considered
- creating pollution and toxic run-off
- burning oil to transport everything around the world.

This is just some of the waste you and I don't see but it has the *biggest* impact. A simple action we can take, like reusing instead of buying new, will help curb this 'upstream' wastefulness.

Your zero-waste lifestyle can follow a framework that can help with decision-making, especially when you're new to this way of thinking. My own personal *Waste Not* framework includes these steps:

1. redesign
2. rethink
3. refuse
4. reduce
5. reuse
6. share
7. repair
8. compost
9. recycle
10. choose kindness
11. be the change.

You'll note that recycling is towards the end. This is because the act of recycling is not the way to fix the problem: instead it simply delays items, especially plastics, from ending up in landfill. Recycling doesn't do anything to tackle the real problem – our wasteful consumption. To learn more about why recycling is not the solution you can read my book *Waste Not: Make a Big Difference by Throwing Away Less*. One of the goals of zero waste is to recycle less too!

To reduce our waste, we have to know what we are throwing into these bins. Sustainability Victoria collated information about the contents of garbage bins of everyday people in my home state and, from the illustration on the next page, you can see what we are throwing away. A peek at similar reports across Australia, the UK and the USA will show that the contents of our bins are similar! You'll see we are still putting recyclables, especially food packaging, into our garbage stream too.

FOOD + ORGANICS — 35.6%

RECYCLABLES — 10.8%

OTHER — 53.6%

BUILDING MATERIALS

NAPPIES

GARDEN MATERIALS

PET LITTER

E-WASTE

HOME HEALTHCARE/HYGIENE

HOUSEHOLD CHEMICALS

CERAMICS/PYREX®/GLASSWARE

EXPANDED POLYSTYRENE

TEXTILES (CLOTHES, CLEANING CLOTHS)

TREATED WOOD

(reference: Victorian Statewide Garbage Bin Audit 2013)

A bin audit will help you see what ends up in your personal household's rubbish. For this exercise, I suggest splitting recyclables into plastics and other packaging so that you can see how much single-use plastic you throw away.

There are two ways to carry out your own bin audit:

1. Find a piece of paper to reuse (by writing on the back) or create an on-screen document and divide it into four sections. Label the sections with these headings: edible food and scraps, plastics (plastic food packaging, bottles, toiletries, etc.), other packaging, and other. Before putting anything into your bin, write the item on the list. Over two weeks you'll quickly see themes emerge. You can do this with your recycling bin too, once you've got your landfill bin pared down.

2. Find a large area and lay down a tarp (if you don't have one, borrow from a neighbour, family or friends). Tip out the contents of your bin onto the tarp the day of bin night and begin sorting into four separate piles: edible food and scraps, plastics (plastic food packaging, bottles, toiletries, etc.), other packaging, and other. You'll need gloves and tongs to help you sort through everything. Write down the items found in each section.

Keep a copy of your bin audit and reduce your waste with the tips in each part of this book. The first three parts target those three core categories of household waste: food and organics, recylables and other materials. The last part offers tips on how to reduce waste beyond what's in your bin.

To start with, remember ...

#1

It's easier to change your habits
if you make it fun. So, have fun!

#2

Never think 'I'm not doing enough'.
Any change you make is a positive one.
Even when you occasionally forget to say
no to a straw, there is always another day
when you can try again. Don't be too
hard on yourself (or others around you)!

#3

Do you have a friend, family member or co-worker who'd be a helpful ally in reducing your waste? Ask them to join in helping you with the 365 tips in this book or tackle a section together.

#4

Focus on what works best for you. Remember that some of these tips might not be quite right for you. Our lives and circumstances are unique and different. Do the best you can, with what you've got and where you are.

PART ONE

#5

Each year, one out of every five shopping bags of vegetables, fruit and bread is put into the bin. This wastage roughly costs us $20 a week or over $1000 per year.

#6

Our farmers work hard to provide our food: let's support their early mornings and long days by making sure we eat what they produce.

#7

Before doing your grocery shopping, write a list, choosing ingredients that can be used over several meals. A list will help to stop you from buying food you don't need.

#8

Use the back of envelopes or scraps of paper to write lists, or use your phone.

#9

Plan the breakfasts, snacks, lunches and dinners you want to cook for the coming week or fortnight. Check your refrigerator, fruit bowl and bread bin so nothing is forgotten or overlooked.

#10

Move food that needs to be eaten to the front of the refrigerator and move fruit to a more visible location so you can be reminded that it needs to be eaten first.

Skip the store-bought dressings
and make a salad dressing at home.

Salad dressing

Ingredients
80ml (2½ fl oz/⅓ cup) olive oil
3 tablespoons lemon juice
1 small garlic clove, crushed
salt and black pepper

How to put it together
1. Combine all ingredients in a glass jar.
2. Put the lid on and shake for 30 seconds.

#12

Bags, wallet, keys and phone – your new mantra when leaving to go shopping. Keep your reusable bags in a visibly accessible area or in your car and look for ones that fit into a pocket or handbag. Using your reusable bags will help save 440 plastic bags per household each year.

#13

Invest in reusable produce bags, made from old sheets, sold in health-food stores or found on Etsy.

#14

Forgot your reusable bag? No problem!
If you left the bags in your car, simply
wheel the trolley out to the car and
load everything into the bags there.
If your bags are still at home, ask the
cashier for some boxes.

#15

Look out for Boomerang Bags or
their equivalents at your local store.
These bags are made from recycled fabric
sewn by volunteers. The bags are left
at stores for people to use when they
forget their own bags and to bring
back for another person to use.

#16

Buy your fruit and vegetables loose.
If plastic-free produce is hard for you to
find, join the #plasticfreeproduce campaign
with activist Anita Horan, who offers
helpful materials on anitahoran.com.

#17

Support local growers at a farmers'
market where you'll typically find fruit,
vegetables and bread without any
plastic packaging. Fewer emissions are
produced in transporting the food, and
you'll get to know the families who
grow it.

#18

Choosing produce that is in season helps the environment because more resources are needed to grow and store out-of-season food; you'll also save money as produce is often marked up when sold out of season.

#19

If you can't make it to a farmers' market, look for fruit and vegetable home-delivery subscription services. The boxes are often reusable and you may be able to ask for no plastic packaging.

#20

If a supermarket is your only option, look for items in metal, glass or cardboard packaging, and buy in larger quantities to minimise packaging.

#21

When I'm finding it hard to buy
ingredients because of my location,
lack of time or money, I ask myself:
Do I really need it? How can I buy
this with the least amount of packaging?
How can the packaging be reused?
Is recycling the packaging worth it?
Can I make it myself?

#22

Locate a bulk store or bulk co-op
in your area through websites like
zerowastehome.com,
trashlesstakeaway.com.au and
local online zero-waste Facebook groups.
Bulk stores and co-ops sell food and
other items without any packaging.

#23

Visit a bulk store. You'll be
surprised by how much they
offer and your packaging will reduce
significantly. The staff can help you
if it's your first time shopping there.

#24

Start asking your local deli, butcher
or bakery to refill your own containers,
but perhaps shop at a time
of day when they are not busy. It could
be their first time for such a request
and they might need some time to figure
out their scales and work out the
weight of what you are buying.

#25

Save money by choosing to shop at a bulk store or bulk co-op: you can save between 10 and 65 per cent at these stores since you are not paying for packaging and advertising with each product.

#26

Co-ops are usually not-for-profit stores run by volunteers; bulk stores are typically a normal business. A co-op is an option for people to buy items in a way that benefits the community.

#27

If you have space, order bulk items directly to your home. Many dried goods can be shipped in paper bags but double-check to see what the packaging is and if the store will take it back for reuse. Call up your nearest bulk store to ask for details.

#28

Bakeries, delis, butchers and fishmongers will also accept customers' cloth bags and containers. This is how our great-grandparents used to shop, so it's not that radical; people still shop like this in many areas around the world today!

#29

Buying a loaf of bread in a reusable cloth bag from a bakery each week will save 52 plastic bags and plastic tags each year. Bread also lasts longer in cloth. Or you can always freeze your bread.

What to take shopping to reduce packaging:

- Cloth bags to carry groceries home, for bread from the bakery, and for collecting fruit and vegetables
- Old plastic containers to collect items like olives or cheese or whatever you'd like from the deli, butcher, fishmonger or even a lolly store
- Glass jars and reusable bags for the bulk store
- Empty household cleaner bottles or other bottles work well for cleaning products at bulk stores too.

FOOD

#31

Save the next glass jar, metal tin
and cardboard box from the recycling bin;
instead think about how you could reuse
it, like for storing food, growing herbs,
saving seeds, making candles or using it as
a vase, a light fixture or for craft projects.

#32

Next time you buy something,
don't ask to have a receipt printed
out, particularly a second credit
card receipt. These are often covered
in BPA (bisphenol A – a chemical
used to manufacture plastic) and
many recycling facilities
don't accept receipts.

#33

Keep the Tupperware® and other
plastic containers you own. Resources
and energy went into making them;
there are many ways to value this
by reusing them in other ways.

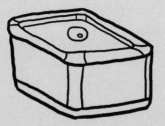

#34

Learn to make the foods that you used to buy prepackaged. Preserving food by canning, and making jam, pasta sauces, dips, bread, pasta, muesli bars and biscuits are some of the many things that you can do at home to help reduce packaging, while also learning a new skill.

Simple three-ingredient crackers

Ingredients
1 cup flour (any flour you want)
herbs, such as rosemary or thyme (optional)
3 tablespoons olive oil
4 tablespoons cold water

How to put it together
1. Preheat oven to 200°C (400°F).
2. Combine flour, herbs (for flavour, if using) and olive oil in a bowl. The mixture will be crumbly.
3. Add the water 1 tablespoon at a time until you get a dough-like consistency. Depending on the flour, you might not need all 4 tablespoons or you may need more.
4. Break the dough up into four equal parts and roll out thin (around 2 mm). I use a pasta machine but a rolling pin or even a wine bottle will do the job.
5. Cut the crackers to a desired shape. Lay them on a baking tray and put into the oven for up to 8 minutes. Check them at 6 minutes. The crackers will be golden and crispy when done.

#36

Store food properly. Carrots, celery
and asparagus can be kept in water to
keep them crisp; tomatoes should be
kept out of the fridge. When our food is
wrapped in plastic, it's more likely to be
forgotten and will go off more quickly too.

#37

To maximise shelf life, keep bread in
a cotton bag and cheese wrapped in
cheese paper or a wax wrap inside a
container in the fridge. Bread will also
last longer when bought unsliced.

#38

Nuts and seeds will last longest
and best if you keep them in the fridge.

#39

Cook root to tip. Cauliflower leaves, beetroot (beet) leaves and stalks, carrot top stalks, coriander (cilantro) stems, pepitas (pumpkin seeds) and potato skins can all be eaten.

#40

Save up any scraps or wilted veg to make broths, stocks or even chutney. Overripe fruit can be turned into jam or compote for dessert and porridge. Turn stale bread into crunchy garlic breadcrumbs and croutons for salads and soups.

#41

Citrus peels can be used for cleaning.

General-purpose citrus cleaner

Ingredients

citrus peels (lemon or orange or both)

vinegar

How to put it together

1. Half fill an empty jar with the citrus peels.
2. Top up the jar with vinegar.
3. Put the lid on and keep in a dark place
for 6 weeks. Strain.
4. Decant to a spray bottle and use.

#42

Become a leftover lover
and package any food left
from the night before to
have for lunch the
next day.

#43

Instead of using plastic wrap for leftovers, swap to plates on top of bowls and glass jars, drape tea (dish) towels over dishes or use wax wraps. Wax wraps are washable and reusable pieces of cotton infused with beeswax – vegan options use soy or candelilla – to create a waterproof barrier.

#44

If you don't want to make something from scratch, like pizza dough or pastry, call a local pizza restaurant or bakery to ask if they will sell you a ready-made option that you can pick up (in your own container, of course).

#45

Grow foods like spinach, silverbeet and salad leaves that supermarkets often sell in plastic. My favourite books for growing in small spaces are *One Magic Square* by Lolo Houbein and *The Edible Balcony* by Indira Naidoo.

#46

Certain edible plants work as natural pest control. Marigolds (calendula) help keep insects from tomatoes and other vegetables, and the flowers can go into salads or homemade beauty balms.

#47

When growing vegetables, don't forget to include some flowers if space permits. The flowers can be used to decorate your home and make lovely gifts for family and friends. Having flowers also supports the ecosystem by encouraging bees, butterflies and birds to visit.

#48

Take the ends with roots attached of spring onion, lettuce, celery, bok choy, fennel, leek or beetroot and place into a container. Cover the roots with water and keep the container on a windowsill. After a week, if the plant begins sprouting new growth, transfer to a pot or the garden.

#49

Save the seeds from pumpkins, tomatoes and eggplants as a package-free way to plant a food garden. You can also try saving seeds from plants after they flower in your garden. Ask family and friends if you can have any of their seeds and share yours with others.

#50

Try growing and drying your own herbs like thyme, oregano, parsley, basil and chives. Mint can be dried for tea. Use sunlight or a dehydrator for drying these and other foods.

#51
Freeze excess herbs and olive oil together in ice cube trays then pop them out to add flavour to dishes. Zest lemon rind before juicing and store it in ice cube trays too.

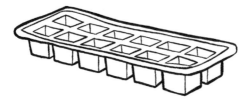

#52

To remove the labels from jars you are reusing, soak in hot water for an hour then remove. Use eucalyptus oil or tea-tree oil and a cloth rag to take off stubborn labels and glue residue.

#53

Check with your local council to see if you can grow food on your nature strip (boulevard). Invite neighbours to get involved too. If you live in an apartment with an accessible rooftop, talk with the body corporate or building manager about the possibility of growing plants on the roof.

#54

Join a harvest swap through apps and websites like ripenear.me to share surplus vegetables, fruit and homemade foods with members of your local community.

#55

Chickens make great pets and also help deal with food scraps while providing manure for your soil.

#56

Try reducing animal consumption by starting with a Meatless Monday or trying homemade oat milk. Linseeds (flax seeds), apple sauce or even bananas make a simple egg substitute.

#57

Visit Gumtree, Craigslist and
Facebook Buy Swap Sell groups
to find secondhand pots and planter
boxes. Try making your own with
reclaimed wood.

#58

Does your community, suburb or
city have a tool library or sharing
shed? Visit them to see what you
can borrow instead of buying. Search
for online platforms that allow you to
hire items for a small fee, or ask
family and friends to see what they
can lend you.

#59

There are garden centres and nurseries that don't sell soil, compost and other garden supplies in plastic bags. You'll need a friend with a trailer (and a vehicle that can tow it) to pick up your unpacked purchases, which you can also shovel into repurposed large bags or crates.

#60

Setting up a compost or worm farm can cut your landfill waste by half. It also helps reduce greenhouse emissions and puts nutrients back into the soil. Bokashi bins are ideal for smaller homes or apartments.

#61

Sites like sharewaste.com allow those who don't have room for their own compost or worm farm to find others in the community who would like to accept food waste (keep food scraps in the freezer between drop-offs to reduce smell).

#62

Weed killer

Ingredients
315 g (11 oz/1 cup) salt
1 litre (34 fl oz/4 cups) vinegar

How to put it together
1. Dissolve the salt in the vinegar.
2. Brush onto weeds carefully, as it
   will also kill other plants.

#63

Weeds and even seaweed can be
collected and used as fertiliser on a
garden. Soak either in water for a week,
drain and use the water as food for
your plants. Then compost what's left.

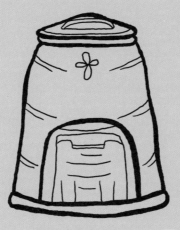

#64

Garden waste like grass clippings, leaves, branches and weeds can be placed into your local council's green bin. If you have a large compost, you can place them in that.

#65

Some councils will even accept other organic waste – like food scraps – in green waste bins, but double-check first by calling or checking their website for details. If they don't offer the service, you can suggest they start.

#66

Swap disposable paper towel for a cloth tea (dish) towel and save 7300 paper towels from being sent to landfill. Then wash your tea towel with a full load of other towels.

#67

Tea bags can contain plastic; this stops the paper from dissolving when the boiling water hits it. Use loose-leaf tea with a teapot and metal strainer. Don't forget to compost the tea leaves.

#68

Swap out single-use coffee pods for a coffee plunger or coffee machine, or look for companies offering reusable coffee pods. Coffee grounds make a great body scrub or can be put into the garden or into pot plants.

#69

Return the excess rubber bands
from your fruit and vegetables to
farmers. This will save on resources
and save them money too.

#70

If you buy fruit or vegetables
in containers at farmers'
markets, see if you can return
the packaging for reuse.

#71

Make your own newspaper bin-liner
from leftover newspapers found at
cafes or the library. Some councils
prefer residents to wrap their rubbish
for collection to stop the risk of
anything escaping into gutters and
ending up in our waterways.

#72

Learn the art of fermenting, pickling
and even drying foods so you can
enjoy your bounty out of season and
reuse some of those glass jars. Check
your local area for classes or ask a
relative to show you how to
get started.

#73

Try making your own dips
like hummus or this avocado
tahini dip instead of buying
a packaged option.

Avocado tahini dip

Ingredients
1 avocado, peeled and stone removed
3 tablespoons fresh lemon juice
½ teaspoon ground cumin
2 tablespoons freshly chopped
coriander (cilantro) leaves
90 g (3 oz/⅓ cup) tahini
60 ml (2 fl oz/¼ cup) water
¼ teaspoon salt

How to put it together
1. Blend ingredients in a food processor
   until well combined and serve.

#74

Try roasting forgotten and limp vegetables with garlic and herbs on a low heat in the oven until cooked, then place inside a sterilised glass jar and fill the jar with olive oil. You'll have a simple dish to pull out and have at a party, and the oil can be reused again.

#75

If you come across a recipe that encourages less food waste, share it on your social media or email it to family and friends, and even colleagues. It's a fun and easy way to spread the message and raise awareness of food waste.

#76

Over 40 per cent of the plastic found in the Great Pacific Garbage Patch is from discarded fishing nets. Think of reducing the amount of fish you eat and only choosing brands that use line and pole.

#77

Make your own yoghurt, even from plant-based milks. Look for tutorials online and classes in your area. If the idea still seems daunting, buy the biggest tub instead of smaller individual tubs.

#78

There is a growing trend of smaller
businesses offering milk and plant-based
milks in returnable glass bottles. Check at
your local farmers' market, the health-food
store and local grocer.

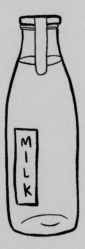

#79

Buy cheese in your own container or buy a wheel to split between friends.

#80

Butter can be found unpackaged at markets: just bring along your own container. Or choose paper-wrapped butter and reuse the paper to line muffin and cake tins.

#81

Share your knowledge on reducing food waste at a local school or community centre. Learning from passionate individuals face-to-face is inspiring and a wonderful way to spread the message offline.

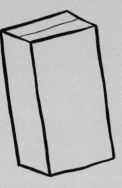

#82

Cardboard boxes collected from local stores can be used as weed matting in your garden instead of using plastic.

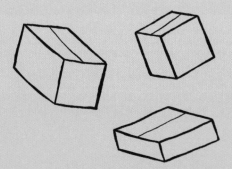

#83

Join a local foraging group in your area to learn what native and wild foods are safe to eat. Finding free food is always fun!

#84

In the lead-up to Christmas, when rubbish increases by more than 50 per cent, start emptying the freezer so you have room to store all the yummy leftovers. Encourage guests to bring along an empty container or lend out some of your own so guests can take any extra food home.

#85

If for some reason you are not able to cook any perishable food you've bought, put a message out on social media to family and friends or into a local Facebook group asking if anyone would like to come and pick it up.

#86

If you are finding it hard to locate unpackaged options, join an online zero-waste community specific to your state or town. Search by looking up 'zero waste town/city/area/state name' and meet with other helpful individuals who are also working towards a world without waste.

PART TWO

#87

Everything we own is special
and should be treated with care, with
the hope of having it forever or
passing it onto someone else
who will find it useful.

#88

Don't be afraid to speak up. Contact
companies to suggest they create
smarter products or more sustainable
packaging. Ask for change from large
businesses by writing letters, sending
emails and making comments on their
social media with simple hashtags like
#breakfreefromplastic.

#89

More than 1 million plastic water
bottles are bought every minute; about
91 per cent of this plastic is NOT recycled.
Imagine the amount of waste caused
by every other plastic bottle in your home.
It's not only our food that is packaged in
too much plastic but also what we use
to clean our home and bodies.

#90

If you do find you need to buy
anything in plastic, consider
supporting brands using recycled
plastic. We are not really recycling if
we aren't buying recycled products.

#91

Become a smart recycler! Each council, state and country recycles differently. The best place to learn what are the correct items to place into your kerb recycling is your local council's website or from whoever manages your recycling.

#92

Websites like recyclingnearyou.com.au in Australia, recycle.co.nz in New Zealand, earth911.com in the USA and recyclenow.com in the UK have information on items that can be recycled but not accepted through your local rubbish collection, like mattresses or light globes.

#93

In the UK alone, more than
4000 tonnes of aluminium foil
is discarded during Christmas festivities.
If foil can't be reused, rinse it and roll it
into a ball the size of your fist so it
can be recycled. Or do without.

#94

Avoid 'wish-cycling' or putting
something into the recycling bin,
hoping for the best. If we get our
recycling wrong or do it through
incorrect collection points, we are
potentially damaging the recycling
process for others who do take the
time to do it correctly.

#95

Look out for new recycling labels on packaging that explain in detail how each part of the materials can or can't be recycled. Detailed recycling information can help us make the right decision and be aware of any sneaky plastic that we might not know about.

#96

Some of the stuff you throw away
as rubbish and recycling could be
reimagined in craft projects for kids
and adults alike. Keep a box aside to
collect what could be used again for
rainy day activities.

#97

Over 1.9 million tonnes of
packaging, the equivalent of filling
the Melbourne Cricket Ground nine
times, is thrown away each
year by Australians.

#98

Forty per cent of plastic
manufactured is for packaging.

#99

Avoid plastic bottles of cordial
and tetra cardboard juice boxes (the
latter can't be recycled). Instead make
cordials and lemonade at home or infuse
water using leftover scraps from meal
prep; store your homemade drinks in
old wine and glass juice bottles.

#100

If you are partial to fizzy drinks, invest in a system so you can carbonate your own.

#101

Search for breweries and wineries in your area or local businesses selling alcohol that offer refills for beer, wine and spirits. Or join a class to learn how to brew at home.

#102

If you are looking to move house, check your local Facebook Marketplace and Gumtree or Craigslist for used moving boxes then pass them on once you've unpacked. Or ask local businesses if you can take some of their used boxes.

#103

Supermarkets stock laundry powders packaged in cardboard without plastic scoops. Reuse a scoop you already have; a tablespoon will work too! By choosing brands like Aware Environmental (Australia), Ecover (UK) and Meliora (USA), you can save up to twelve plastic scoops a year!

REUSE ME!

#104

Collect the ends of soap bars to make your own liquid soap for handwashing or woolwash.

Handwash and woolwash

Ingredients
2 tablespoons soap ends
750 ml (25½ fl oz/3 cups) water

How to put it together
1. Add soap ends to a pot and cover with the water.
2. Bring to a boil on the stove for 5 minutes, reduce heat to low and simmer for another 15 minutes, stirring throughout.
3. Once soap ends have dissolved, let the mixture cool and pour into a bottle.

#105

Soap nuts, available at most bulk
and health-food stores, are a compostable
and budget-friendly alternative to
laundry powders and liquids.

#106

If you live in a region where horse
chestnuts grow, these can also be
collected and turned into free
homemade soap.

#107

A bottle of simple white vinegar is more effective than half the products in supermarket cleaning aisles. Use it to clean away grease, bacteria and mould; a dash even works as a fabric softener. A vinegar-soaked cloth makes for a reusable dryer sheet if air-drying clothes is not an option.

#108

We're often sold the idea we need one cleaning spray for the kitchen, another for the bathroom, another for glass and another for tiles. Think about all the resources needed to make each container and pump; reduce your waste by buying your products from a bulk store or by simply buying less. You can even try making your own cleaning products.

#109

Spray-and-wipe cleaner

Ingredients
bar of soap (grated, remainder kept
in glass jar for future use)
2 litres (68 fl oz/8 cups) hot water
1 drop tea-tree oil

How to put it together
1. Add 1 teaspoon of grated soap
to the hot water.
2. Add a drop of tea-tree oil.
3. Decant to a spray bottle to use.

#110

Avoid mops with replaceable pads that get used once then thrown away; use a regular mop and bucket instead.

#111

Stay away from brightly coloured synthetic cleaning cloths and brushes. Upcycle towels and cotton shirts as cleaning cloths and choose other natural options that can break down in your compost: scouring pads made from coconut husks and wooden-handled brushes with replaceable heads.

#112

Liquid washes are mostly water. Instead of buying separate bottles of face wash, body wash, hand wash and dishwashing liquid, replace them all with a bar of unpackaged soap or one bought in paper. That's four plastic bottles saved!

#113

Look in the garden for simple ingredients that can be used for beauty, cleaning and home remedies, such as aloe vera, roses, lavender, nettle, rosemary, thyme, sage, mint, calendula, violets and chamomile.

#114

Look to the kitchen for simple and affordable homemade beauty ingredients: honey, salt, vinegar, bicarbonate of soda (baking soda), citrus, oils, sugar and herbs.

#115

Clove oil kills mould and can
be used to make toothpaste; tea-tree
oil is a disinfectant; eucalyptus oil is
anti-microbial, can treat stains and
remove sticky labels; and lavender
will help repel insects and is anti-bacterial.
Only a little is needed of each for any
use, so they will last a long time.

#116

Making your own beauty and
home cleaning products with safe
ingredients will help reduce our
exposure to potentially toxic products.
We only have two homes: the earth and
our body. Let's take care of each
with kindness.

#117

Many of the ingredients in
homemade cleaning and beauty items
have multiple uses. For instance, bicarbonate
of soda (baking soda) can be used for
toothpaste, cleaning and cooking. Vinegar
is used for cleaning and cooking. Beeswax
goes into a lip balm, furniture polish
and shoe polish.

#118

Shampoo and hair conditioner
are available at bulk stores. Take
your own bottles, either your old ones
or another container, and fill up.

#119

Shampoo and conditioner can also
be bought in solid form, similar to
a bar of soap, with no or minimal
paper-based packaging. These shampoo
bars can be found at health stores,
bulk stores, some mainstream stores,
such as Lush, and even pharmacies.

#120

A paste of bicarbonate of soda
(baking soda) or rye flour and water,
followed by a rinse with apple cider
vinegar or rosemary tea, are a few low-waste
methods people use to keep their hair
clean, including the author of this book!

#121

Swap store-bought dry shampoo for
a homemade version with tapioca or
arrowroot flour, adding cocoa for darker
hair colours. Both flours can also be used
as a face powder to control shine too.

#122

Make a hydrating hair mask
using a variety of ingredients such
as bananas, aloe vera gel, eggs, oils,
linseeds (flax seeds) or honey.

#123

Linseeds (flax seeds) can be made
into a hair gel that will replace the
packaged store-bought equivalent.

#124

Keep your haircuts low waste by
choosing a sustainable salon (in
Australia or New Zealand) with
sustainablesalons.org.

#125

Hair and nail clippings can be put into your compost.

#126

Sea salt texturising hair spray

Ingredients
1 tablespoon sea salt (or ordinary salt)
½ tablespoon bicarbonate of soda (baking soda)
250 ml (8½ fl oz/1 cup) hot water

How to put it together
1. Mix all ingredients until the salt and bicarbonate of soda are dissolved.
2. Pour into a spray bottle and use.

#127

Every plastic toothbrush ever manufactured still exists somewhere today. When it's time to buy a new brush, try one made of bamboo or wood. These come with removable nylon bristles, so the handle can be composted or upcycled into a garden marker.

#128

Used plastic toothbrushes can be recycled at TerraCycle – see TerraCycle's website for your country: terracycle.com.au in Australia, terracycle.co.nz in New Zealand, terracycle.co.uk in the UK and terracycle.com in the USA – or you can reuse them at home to assist with cleaning.

Toothpaste tubes are accepted through TerraCycle too, or you can try tooth tabs. These can be bought in glass, cardboard or returnable plastic. You can also make a simple toothpaste.

Clove and sweet orange toothpowder

Ingredients
5 tablespoons bicarbonate of soda
(baking soda)
5 drops clove oil
10 drops sweet orange oil
2–4 tablespoons coconut oil (optional)

How to put it together
1. Combine the bicarbonate of soda, clove oil and sweet orange oil in a jar.
2. Seal with the lid and shake vigorously.
3. Add 2–4 tablespoons of coconut oil to make into a paste.

#130

Look for dental floss made of compostable silk packaged in a refillable glass holder, such as the brand Dental Lace. Water picks and oil pulling are two alternative low-waste options.

#131

Over 255 billion facial tissues are used each year in the USA. That's a lot of trees! Cotton handkerchiefs can be washed after use and will not only save on the trees and water needed to make disposable tissues but also the packaging.

#132

Most cotton buds are made with a plastic stick. Ditch the plastic-stemmed cotton buds for ones that use wood, and compost them rather than putting into landfill.

#133

Swapping packaged pads and tampons for reusable period underwear, cloth pads or silicone menstrual cups will not only reduce what goes into your bathroom bin but also save money.

#134

There is a growing number of toilet paper brands like Who Gives a Crap and Pure Planet making tree-free toilet paper and packaging in paper only. The paper wrapping can be reused before it's placed in the recycling bin.

#135

Thirty years ago, Americans were throwing out 2 billion plastic razors each year – that's at least 60 billion discarded since then. Swap to a safety razor, where only the blades need to be replaced and are recyclable. Use a shaving soap bar instead of the foaming packaged option.

#136

Do you smell? You might find
that you don't smell that bad
without deodorant. Changing your
clothes from synthetic fibres to natural
will help reduce underarm odour.
Try a splash of apple cider vinegar diluted
with water, make your own deodorant
or look for brands in
metal and glass containers.

Bicarbonate of soda deodorant

Ingredients

¼ cup bicarbonate of soda (baking soda)
¼ cup arrowroot, tapioca or cornstarch
1½ to 2 tablespoons coconut oil
10 drops tea-tree oil (optional)

How to put it together

1. Mix the bicarbonate of soda and arrowroot (or alternatives) in a bowl.
2. Add the coconut oil and tea-tree oil (if using). Start with 1½ tablespoons of the coconut oil; add more if you want a runnier paste.
3. Scoop the mixture into a sterilised wide-mouth glass jar.
4. Store in a cool dark place for up to a year.
5. To use, scoop a pea-size amount for each underarm and wipe over area.

#138

Perfume bottles contain a lot
of different materials in their packaging,
which make them hard to recycle. Try
making your own by adding a couple of
drops of your favourite essential oils to
a carrier oil, like sunflower or grapeseed,
and for bonus points, use a
reusable roller bottle.

#139

In 2008, the cosmetics industry
created over 210 billion units of
packaging. Not million – *billion*. Most
of this was not recycled and a lot of
the packaging was plastic.

#140

Keep empty make-up containers
like mascara tubes and eyeshadow
palettes out of the rubbish bin and
look up TerraCycle in your country to
find local drop-off points where they
can be collected and recycled. You
or your workplace might even become
inspired to become a collection point.

#141

Instead of recycling cosmetics
jars and containers, keep them for
your homemade beauty and cleaning
products for yourself or as gifts.

#142

Oils make a great low-waste beauty swap from the moisturisers we've been told we need. One oil can replace conditioner, face cream, eye cream, body cream, hand cream, foot cream ... that's a lot of packaging being saved too!

#143

Oil is not only a moisturiser; it also works for removing make-up and cleansing the face. Use a warm washcloth instead of disposable and biodegradable wipes.

#144

Balance the natural pH of your
skin with apple cider vinegar diluted
with water as a simple homemade toner.

#145

Exfoliate with ingredients from your
kitchen that also act as a face mask.
Explore online how to use sugar,
oatmeal, honey, apple cider vinegar,
lemon, ground coffee and even papaya
in beauty products.

#146

Etsy, local markets, health-food stores and bulk stores stock ready-made zero-waste beauty products and ingredients for making your own.

#147

Lip balm

Ingredients
2 tablespoons beeswax
6 tablespoons olive oil

How to put it together
1. Fill a saucepan with water and place a glass bowl on top as a double boiler, bringing the heat of the stove to medium.
2. Put the beeswax and olive oil into the glass bowl and stir until the beeswax has melted and both have combined. Pour into a container or old lip balm tin and leave to cool before using.

#148

Do your personal care products contain plastic microbeads? Due to their size, microbeads escape into lakes and oceans where they are consumed by wildlife. Beat the Microbead is an app that lets you scan a product's barcode while shopping to find out if it contains microbeads.

#149

If you don't have access to bulk stores or prefer not to make your own cleaning or personal care products, then choose cardboard, metal or glass packaging. Could you then reuse a metal tin or glass jar before recycling it? Ask the company if the containers can be returned for refill.

#150

According to the Environmental Working Group (EWG), on average women are exposed to 168 synthetic chemicals each day and men to 85. The EWG's Skin Deep database lets us search the ingredients in cosmetics to better understand what is going onto our bodies and into our homes.

#151

Plastics contain hormone-disrupting chemicals such as phthalates and BPA (bisphenol A, often replaced by bisphenol S). These are released into the liquids and food in plastic containers at warmer temperatures. They can be found in kids' toys and cosmetics as well as food containers.

#152

Part of reducing waste is rethinking not only the packaging but also what's inside it. Most shampoos and household cleaners stocked at bulk stores have fewer harmful ingredients and are safer for the environment since these stores usually have an environmental and health focus.

#153

Our wellbeing is linked with the health of the planet. Keeping our environment healthy will help keep us healthy too.

#154

The air quality inside our homes
is important and keeping plants like
Boston ferns, peace lilies and spider
plants will help absorb toxic chemicals
like formaldehyde from indoor air.

#155

The number one item littered
on beaches is cigarette butts. Instead
of being thrown out, cigarettes and
their packaging can be recycled
through a TerraCycle program (see
the website in your country). Or
perhaps consider giving up smoking ...

#156

Let's not be tempted to measure
our progress to reduce what's in
our bins by comparing ourselves to
past choices or those of other people.
Instead, use your energy to focus
on building a new story with a
happy ending.

#157

If you are feeling overwhelmed with
trying to reduce your waste and
finding some areas harder than others,
don't get down on yourself. Trying our
best is better than not trying at all.

#158

Reducing our rubbish footprint and valuing resources is not the only goal of a zero-waste life; it's also about simplifying what we need and how much we buy, and choosing moments over material items.

#159

A zero-waste life is also about
checking the ingredients we use; one
to avoid is palm oil due to the deforestation,
animal destruction and community
displacement caused by its production.
Palm oil isn't even needed. Look up
palmoilinvestigations.org to find out
if it's in your products.

#160

Living a zero-waste life can help
save money. If you are able to, invest
some of that money into environmental
projects within the local community.

#161

By 2050, the ocean will contain more plastic by weight than fish if we don't start making changes today.

#162

Don't let scary statistics weigh
you down; channel that energy into
changes you can make in your home
or community. Joining with like-minded
individuals can help remind us there is
a growing group of people who imagine
choices being made with kindness and
not at the expense of others.

Five single-use plastics to swap out ...

Most of these plastics are
the ones we see each other using
outside the house. When people begin
seeing us publicly refusing single-use
plastics, this will help actively get
others on board. To help make the
switch, use your phone calendar app
to add reminders that will pop up
before you do your weekly shop, put
notes around the house and put your
new reusables in a visible location
so you can grab them easily if you
are running late – especially while
you are learning these new
plastic-free habits.

Along with the plastic lid, single-use coffee cups are often lined with a sneaky plastic and usually end up in landfill. Take ten minutes to sit down to have your hot drink in a regular ceramic cup, invest in a reusable to-go cup made of glass or grab a mug from the office kitchen. Ask if you can have a discount for bringing your own cup too.

If you can, say no to straws. When the waiter takes your order ask them to write down your request for no straw. Some drinks might call for straws, so why not invest in a reusable straw made of either bamboo, stainless steel, silicone or glass?

Researchers have discovered one plastic bag in the ocean can break apart into 1.75 million separate microscopic pieces. Human beings managed to do the shopping without plastic bags for hundreds of years. Swap out for a reusable cloth tote, wicker basket or your own trolley.

Pull out your Tupperware® or invest in stainless steel and pyrex® containers that can be reused when buying your takeaway lunch or picking up olives from the deli. Those takeaway plastic containers split easily. Avoid the single-use plastic cutlery for an added bonus!

With a reusable bottle tucked away in your bag you will save money and realise how silly paying for bottled water is. Why pay for something you can get from a tap or refilled at a cafe?

PART THREE

#163

The majority of items in the 'other materials' section of your bin audit are modern inventions – disposable nappies, school supplies, electronics, household chemicals. The suggestions in this section will have you thinking, 'Hey, my grandparents or great-grandparents lived like this.' Remember, human beings survived and thrived for a long time without creating the amount of rubbish we make today.

#164

Entertaining? Instead of single-use plastic or paper versions, choose real plates, cutlery and glassware already in your home. If you need more, ask family and friends to lend items, or purchase extras from a local charity store. Ask guests to bring their own picnic sets to an outdoor barbecue.

#165

You don't need brand-new party decorations to make an event fun. See what secondhand stores have on offer or get crafty and make your own using natural options (which can be composted afterwards) foraged from the garden or your local area.

#166

Avoid plastic lighters
and choose wooden matches in
cardboard boxes. You can put the
used sticks into your home compost
or let them burn away.

#167

Glitter and some confetti are
made of plastic. It can easily escape
into the wider environment, where animals
mistake it for food. Think about going
without, otherwise look for glitter made from
natural minerals (such as mica or cellulose)
or use a hole punch to make confetti
out of dried leaves.

#168

Swap paper invitations and envelopes
for digital ones using an online invitation
platform, such as Greenvelope. If you
prefer physical invitations, choose 100 per cent
post-consumer recycled paper or
recycle paper at home to make your
own paper and envelopes.

#169

Don't stress if guests bring plastic-wrapped or packaged food. They might not know about your waste-reduction aims and only want to share a meal with you. Let guests know ahead of time, have beeswax wraps out or share a social media tip about avoiding plastic wrap and over-packaged items.

If you find yourself at a party
with disposable plates, cutlery and
cups, ask the host if you can use a real
plate and cutlery from their cupboards,
offering to wash it up afterwards. Explain
politely that you are simply trying to
cut down on the rubbish you make.

#171

Instead of sending a thank-you card
for a gift or an event, pick up the
phone to thank your host.

#172

Balloons are used once. When they escape into the environment, they pose a serious threat to wildlife, especially birds. Look for balloons made of felt, or paper decorations and bunting that can be reused over and over. Bubbles are a fun option too.

#173

Choose a local native tree for Christmas that can be kept in a pot and reused each year. If you already own a plastic tree, then the sustainable option is to continue using it.

#174

Make your own Christmas crackers
using empty toilet rolls, salvaged
tissue paper and your own jokes. Make
Christmas hats from newspaper or
recycled gift wrap. If you want to buy
a gift, see what can be found at
a secondhand store.

#175

More than half of Australians –
53 per cent – have admitted to throwing
away a Christmas gift.

#176

Before buying a gift, ask the
following questions: Does this person
really need it? Is this a useful gift?
What will happen at the end of the
gift's life? Can it be repaired, reused,
recycled or will it end up in landfill?

#177

When it comes to buying gifts remember the 5H rule: handmade, homemade, healthy, helpful and here (made locally in your area).

BORROW OR HIRE

FIX WHAT'S
BROKEN

BUY SECONDHAND

USED

MAKE YOURSELF

JAM

RECEIPT

$$$

BUY NEW
(AS A LAST RESORT)

#178
There are different ways to shop for new things. Let's redefine buying brand-new as being brand-new to us, not never used before!

USE WHAT YOU HAVE

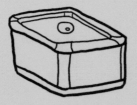

#179

Have a rummage through your jewellery box or kitchen cupboards for items you like but don't use. Clean them up and regift them to someone who will use them.

#180

There are many gifts worth giving that are meaningful and don't create clutter: a night out at the movies with dinner, a gift voucher for a month of coffees at a favourite cafe, walking someone's dog for a month, concert and theatre tickets, skateboard lessons and cooking classes for kids.

#181

Wrap gifts with cloth bags, secondhand scarves, tea (dish) towels or leftover fabric from sewing. Look up furoshiki, a Japanese style of wrapping using cloth. Not only does it look cool, the reusable cloth wrapping will be a conversation starter on using less paper.

#182

Vintage magazines (from charity stores), newspaper, atlas pages, old street directories and even children's artwork make great wrapping instead of buying new rolls of wrapping paper for each celebration.

Try making your own decorative patterns with stamps made from potatoes and experimenting with homemade inks from vegetables and fruit like beetroot (beets) for a fun craft project.

OTHER

#184

Most plastic tape is not recycled. Instead use compostable twine, wool or ribbons for gift wrapping. Homemade glue is also a simple zero-waste option for holding wrapping paper together.

Homemade glue

Ingredients
1 tablespoon flour
water

How to put it together
1. Mix the flour and a small amount of water to form a paste.
2. Use a paintbrush to paint the glue onto the paper you need to stick together.

#185

Make gift tags using the front of old Christmas or birthday cards, use foraged leaves or visit a secondhand store to see what they have in their craft section.

#186

Flowers are classic decorations for any event that can be composted after use. But often they are imported, creating a large environmental footprint. Support the local floristry industry by asking for local and seasonal flowers only, without plastic wrapping and bags.

#187

Overflowing bins, including our recycling bins, enable plastic to end up in our waterways, where it becomes a magnet for DDT, dioxins, industrial fallout, heavy metals and other nasties. Fish eat the plastic coated with these harmful chemicals, which then make their way up the food chain to our plates!

#188

The expanded polystyrene used for packaging generally can't be put in your recycling bin. Before buying something you think could come packaged in polystyrene, ask for your item to be sent without or for the business to accept it back for reuse. Search online for specialist recycling options in your area.

#189

There will be certain products
that can be hard to find without
packaging, like sunscreen and medicines.
Always make decisions that are best
for your health and wellbeing. Just
remember to recycle correctly and
dispose of medication at collection
points like the pharmacy.

#190

Ask your eye-care supplier if
they accept disposable contact lenses
and the blister packaging for recycling.
If they don't, suggest they partner
with TerraCycle to help capture and
recycle in the future.

#191

Kooshoo hair ties are made of 75 per cent organic cotton and 25 per cent natural rubber, instead of synthetics. If you're feeling adventurous, look out for hair ties on the footpath. Once you've seen one, you'll see them all the time and you'll never need to buy them again. Just boil them to remove any germs.

#192

Make a swap to a wooden hairbrush
when yours breaks or if you need to buy
one new. Make sure to support companies
that practise sustainable forest
management.

#193

Landfills are full of dangerous chemicals from cleaning products, discarded batteries, paints, pesticides, plastics and electronics to name a few. The chemicals can enter our groundwater and escape through the air.

#194

Grass clippings, tree branches and weeds should be kept out of landfill. Make sure they are placed in a compost bin or taken to a drop-off point where they are accepted. Organic matter doesn't break down properly in landfill.

#195

Don't send paint, deck stains or shellacs to landfill; instead check to see if there are programs like Paintback in your area that collect used paint for responsible disposal and innovative reuse.

#196

Avoid the chemical-laden drain cleaners in plastic bottles labelled 'POISON' and use vinegar, bicarbonate of soda (baking soda) and a plunger.

#197

Gas canisters are one of the top ten items that contaminate recycling bins and they shouldn't be put into landfill bins either. Empty bottles can be refilled many times, swapped at your local service station, returned to the manufacturer or dropped off at a local waste collection point.

#198

Treated timber shouldn't be placed in your landfill or recycling bin, burnt or used for mulch or compost. It requires safe disposal at a licensed landfill site as it contains chemicals that can be harmful to the environment and our health.

#199

When your old washing-up gloves need replacing, try 100 per cent FSC-certified rubber gloves that can be put into your home compost.

#200

Keep broken crockery like
ceramic kitchen plates, bowls and
mugs aside, and break up into smaller
pieces for use in an outdoor mosaic or
as drainage in pots. Reusing the pieces
gives them another life.

#201

Broken drinking glasses shouldn't
go into a recycling bin as they are
made from tempered glass, which is
different from a glass jam jar. One piece
of tempered glass can ruin glass recycling.

Electronic waste is one of the fastest growing waste streams in Australia. Some examples of electronic waste include: TVs, computers, cables, lamps, phones and digital cameras.

When mobile phones go to landfill, they can potentially leach hazardous chemicals into the surrounding environment. Either donate to a local charity or learn about take-back schemes through recyclingnearyou.com.au (Australia), recyclenow.com (UK) and earth911.com (USA).

OTHER

#204

Old IT equipment like desktops, laptops, computer mouses, monitors, printers, scanners, disks, keyboards, CD drives, printed circuit boards, motherboards and network cards can be recycled through IT recycling programs in Australia at stores like Officeworks.

#205

Millions of ink cartridges are thrown into landfill each year. Save money and the environment by refilling them through stores like Cartridge World.

#206

Safely dispose of potentially hazardous household chemicals such as nail polish remover, cleaning products, automotive and building products, glues and fluorescent globes through a Household Chemical CleanOut event, usually organised annually through local waste management services.

#207

Next time you need to get new batteries, invest in rechargeable batteries and a battery recharge system. Rechargeable batteries can be recharged around 1000 times.

#208

Set up bins correctly in your home with labels – organics, soft plastics, recycling – so everything is disposed of properly. This is especially handy when you have family and friends visiting. Go further and keep small containers to collect things like scrap paper or batteries.

#209

If you have pets like dogs or cats, they require a separate compost for their waste. Look up the Tumbleweed pet-poo-only compost or build your own.

#210

If you pick up after your dog three times a day, that's 1095 plastic bags in landfill each year. Instead use old newspaper or a small pail and shovel to collect for your pet compost.

#211

Switch from store-bought silica-, clay- or sand-based kitty litter to dirt or sawdust that can be collected unpackaged and composted at home. There are also brands using recycled paper and walnut shell waste that can be used for other pets too.

#212

Check with your local pet store to see if they sell unpackaged pet food in bulk. If not, buying the biggest bag and reusing the packaging is the next best option.

#213

Ask the butcher for bones for your pets to chew on in a reusable bag or container.

#214

Make your own pet food. Visit your local library for books that teach you how or look online for recipes.

#215

Pet collars can get lost, so instead of the plastic options look for ones made of natural materials just in case.

#216

Keep fleas at bay by making your own spray.

Flea spray for dogs

Ingredients
lemon rind

water

How to put it together
1. Boil equal parts lemon rind covered with water in a saucepan.
2. Simmer on low for 20 minutes, then cool, strain and transfer to a glass spray bottle.
3. Work onto dog's coat and brush through.

#217

Choose pet toys made of natural materials like cotton, hemp and wool that will break down naturally in a home compost.

#218

Sprinkling bicarbonate of soda (baking soda) on pet bedding and airing it outside will help reduce its smell.

#219

Open doors and windows instead of using over-packaged air fresheners that emit worrying chemicals. Or make your own.

Air freshener

Ingredients
½ teaspoon vinegar
150 ml (5 fl oz) water
essential oil of your choice,
like eucalyptus or lavender

How to put it together
1. Mix vinegar and water.
2. Add just a few drops of the essential oil.
3. Pour into a spray bottle to use.

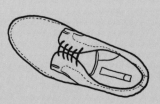

#220

Before bringing something new into your life, pause and think if you really need it. Give yourself two weeks and if you can't stop thinking about buying the item, then buy it. You'll be surprised how much you buy is on impulse.

#221

When you buy from a secondhand store you're not only supporting the circular economy, your money will be used to support programs that help provide food, shelter, skills training and care for those doing it tough. Supporting the circular economy while giving back – yes, please!

#222

If you are feeling inspired to declutter unwanted items from the home, look at other ways to rehome them beyond the hard-rubbish collection or charity store drop-off (they are inundated with stuff). Ask yourself if you could fix it, repurpose it or if anyone you know might need it.

#223

When donating to charity stores, drop items off during opening hours; never leave them at the door overnight. Call first to see if what you are donating is absolutely needed. Charity stores are forced to export excess donations or send them to landfill, costing them valuable funds.

#224

Don't declutter in haste unless you are sure you don't need the items. Store them in a box for two months. If you reach for them during that time, they are probably still of use to you.

#225

When sending anything to a charity store, make sure it's in a condition you would buy: clean, working well and good quality.

#226

For a circular economy to flourish we need to ask companies to take more responsibility rather than have it all fall on the customer's shoulders. With a simple phone call or email, you can find out whether a company accepts items for refill or recycling, or at least plant the idea.

#227

When buying online, use the comments section or send a follow-up email requesting no plastic packaging and suggesting the company reuse old boxes and newspaper as filling instead of synthetic packaging.

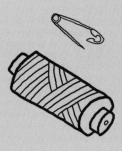

#228

Repairing provides jobs and keeps skills alive. Participating in repairing also puts value on the hours and skills someone spent making the item. If we don't get our things repaired, then the companies who make our stuff won't make them with repairing in mind.

#229

Enrol in a mending or repair
class to learn the skills and confidence
to fix your stuff and help give it a longer
life. If there are no classes available in
your area, make a suggestion to your local
council to run one or search classes
and tutorials online.

#230

If you have mended something and your fix is visible, don't feel discouraged. You are part of the visible mending movement! Check out the hashtag #visiblemending for inspiring visible repairs.

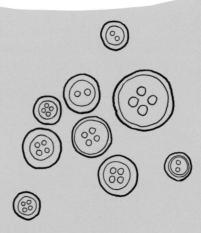

#231

There are a variety of ways to get our stuff repaired. Ask relatives and friends first, with a simple question on social media or a phone call. Search repaircafe.org to see if there is a local group set up near you.

#232

If your product was sold without a repair manual but you need one, email the company or search their website as they might have it available for download. Visit ifixit.com for repair manuals and help on how to fix everyday items.

#233

Each year more than 500,000 tonnes
of textiles end up in Australian landfill.
At the end of each season, check the
soles of shoes, hems of clothes, buttons
and zips to see if they need to be mended
to extend their use for many years to come.

#234

Rather than buy a new gown or suit for
a big event, ask to borrow from a friend
or hire from businesses like Glam Corner,
Rent the Runway and Girl Meets Dress.

#235

Organise a clothing swap with friends,
at work or within the community and have
fun shopping your friends' wardrobes. Turn
the swap into a party with drinks and food.

#236

If your clothing is beyond repair,
consider if it can be upcycled and turned
into something new. For inspiration, check
out kuttlefish.com and the magazine
Junkies. With a bit of imagination,
anything can be upcycled and its
value extended.

#237

Some textiles like worn clothes can
be collected to be reused as rags and
recycled into more fabric. Check with
recyclingnearyou.com.au (Australia),
recycle.co.nz (New Zealand),
earth911.com (USA)
and recyclenow.com (UK)
to find drop-off locations.

#238

Over 90 per cent of clothing worn by Australians is made overseas and shipped here wrapped in individual plastic bags and on coathangers.

#239

Worldwide we consume 80 billion pieces of clothing each year yet we wear only 30 per cent of our wardrobe. Break the cycle of fast fashion by buying less clothing, caring for what you own, shopping secondhand and supporting ethical and locally made clothing made of natural fibres.

#240

Support clothing labels that have a zero-waste ethos. When people ask about what you are wearing, you have an opportunity to share information about why we need to rethink plastic or reduce our obsession with fast fashion. It's wearable activism!

#241

When dropping off your clothes at an eco-drycleaner that doesn't use PERC (perchloroethylene), bring along a reusable dry-cleaning bag and ask for no new plastic wrap.

#242

Nearly all – 82 per cent – of the
energy footprint a garment will create is
in the washing and drying we do each
week, without even factoring in the amount
of water we use. Spot cleaning and turning
clothes inside out to air between wears
will help cut your washing by half.

#243

Our clothes release microfibres
when washed. As many washing machines
and water treatment plants can't filter
them out, they move into waterways.
Natural fibres like cotton break
down but synthetic fibres like polyester
(a type of plastic) won't break down,
increasing plastic pollution.

#244

Plastic clothes pegs can break easily; once broken, they can't be recycled and are hard to repair. Opt for stainless steel pegs that can be recycled when broken beyond repair or wooden pegs that can go into the home compost.

#245

Choose a linen tablecloth that you can wash and reuse for another event instead of the single-use plastic variety.

#246

Babies and children grow quickly.
Instead of buying new clothes, ask
family and friends for any they are ready
to pass on or visit the local secondhand
store, then regift once your children
have outgrown them. The same
goes for maternity clothing, which
is only worn for a short time.

#247

Borrowing, sharing or choosing
secondhand goods saves money, keeps
items from landfill, avoids new plastic,
invests in the circular economy and
values the effort and resources that
went into making the item in the
first place.

#248

Instead of buying gifts for a new baby, focus instead on the wellbeing of the new parent. Cook meals that can be easily frozen, buy a voucher for a nappy cleaning service or a relaxing massage, or offer to look after the baby or tidy the house while the parents sleep in or shower.

#249

Skip the plastic and silicone dummies (soothers) for rubber ones. Natural rubber is biodegradable in a home compost and comes from trees that are a renewable resource.

#250

Reusable breast pads made of cotton can be put into the washing machine, and reused for breastfeeding and saved or passed on to another mother.

#251

When it comes to rehoming baby items, consider charity organisations that collect prams, cots, toys and clothing for families suffering hardships. Ask the community maternal health nurse for specific groups.

#252

Turn a mason jar into a baby
bottle by simply adding a nipple
from Mason Bottle. You can continue
to use it as a jar once your child is
finished with bottle-feeding.

#253

Instead of plastic plates and cups
that can crack when knocked off the
highchair, choose stainless steel or wood.
The stainless steel won't break and the wood
can at least be composted, unlike the
plastic items that cannot be recycled
or broken down.

#254

Try baby-led weaning instead of reaching for the ready-made purees in squeezable pouches or single-use containers. The idea is to let your baby eat the same food as you with their hands to help them understand texture and taste. You can learn more about baby-led weaning from books and guides, but always consult your doctor or maternal health nurse before feeding your baby solids.

#255

You don't need a new bin to keep nappies in before washing them; instead look for a secondhand bucket.

#256

Don't be fooled into thinking that wet wipes and make-up wipes will break down when flushed in the toilet. Instead they clog sewers, costing millions of dollars in sewer maintenance fees each year.

#257

After plastic bags, nappies are often the top item to contaminate recycling bins. Cloth nappies have come a long way, and modern cloth nappies (MCNs) are easy to use and clean; you'll find them in an array of fun patterns too.

#258

If you are thinking of trying cloth nappies but are unsure where to start, look into joining a cloth nappy library. This allows families to hire a range of nappies so they can then choose what works best for them and their baby.

#259

Reusable cloth wipes made of cotton flannel and dampened with water make an easy zero-waste baby cleaning option that will last for more than one child. Having cloth wipes on hand is also good for keeping hands and faces clean too.

#260

Swapping two disposable nappies and six disposable wipes a week for reusable cloth nappies and wipes will prevent 104 disposable nappies and 312 disposable wipes per year going into landfill.

#261

Keep food at kids' parties simple.
Stick to things they can grab easily
as they run around with their friends:
unpackaged food like popcorn, cupcakes,
homemade dips and crackers,
sandwiches, fresh fruit and lollies.
Look out for old-fashioned lolly stores
that offer unpackaged sweets.

#262

Avoid plastic-packaged food dyes. Colour your cakes with natural dyes from your kitchen: red (beetroot juice), green (spinach or spirulina), orange (carrot juice), blue (blueberry juice), yellow (pinch of turmeric dissolved in water) and purple (fresh blackberry juice).

#263

Plastic party bags filled with plastic-covered treats and toys can be swapped for a brown paper bag with homemade unpackaged treats or a small tree to plant. Or rebel: just give everyone a slice of cake in a handmade newspaper container. You don't have to provide party bags, even if others do.

#264

Party games can be low waste,
such as musical statues; big buckets of
water and reusable knitted water balloons;
and pass-the-parcel using fabric and string
instead of paper and plastic tape,
with gifts like crayons or chocolate
wrapped in paper.

#265

Instead of constantly buying new toys,
join a local toy library. You and your
kids can go 'shopping' at the toy library
every few weeks, saving clutter in your
home and money too. Plus it teaches
children to care for toys since they
are sharing them with others.

#266

Making use of local parks and play equipment will cut back the need to buy outdoor toys for your home and also encourage the family to get out of the house. It'll provide fun opportunities to connect with people from the community while getting fresh air.

#267

Instead of buying a new school uniform, ask the school if they have secondhand uniforms for sale.

#268

Avoid the plastic wrap for schoolbooks and use brown paper instead.

#269

Look for lunchboxes – for children and adults – made of stainless steel or another durable material that will last a long time. Ones with different compartments make it easier to carry a variety of food unpackaged. Don't forget to check secondhand stores and online too.

#270

Investigate local Asian retailers for Indian tiffin boxes and Japanese bento boxes. Our diverse multicultural community practises many plastic-free traditions that we can learn from.

#271

Suggest a 'nude food' challenge at school – or work. This is when children – or your colleagues – bring their food without any packaging. It could be for a month – 'Nude November' – or a designated day of the week to get started.

#272

When buying a school backpack,
check to see if it comes with a
warranty so it can be repaired should
a hole appear or zipper break.

#273

At the end of each school year,
ask the teacher at your local school
to keep leftover stationery to be used
the following year, instead of
buying new.

#274

Foster a love for upcycling in
children by encouraging them to use
their imagination to reimagine items
that would otherwise go in the bin.

#275

Invite the household to a park, beach
or walk through a local neighbourhood.
Point out rubbish and ask questions like:
How might they feel about picking up
after someone else? Is there a way to
stop rubbish getting into the environment?
Who or what could this rubbish affect?

#276

Remember to avoid overwhelming
yourself and your family by trying to
make changes quickly. Keep a pace
that works well for your life while
keeping it fun.

#277

Help children understand and learn about the effects of single-use plastics and waste through books, movies and television shows like *Dirt Girl, Wall-E* and Pamela Allen's *A Bag and a Bird*. Visit an exhibition or environmental festival.

#278

Raising young eco-warriors might be hard at times. Lead by example and gently guide them by making it interesting for them. Explain that you are trying to make changes not to create a harder life for them now, but to protect the world for their future.

OTHER

PART FOUR

BEYOND YOUR BIN: WASTE IN THE WIDER WORLD

#279

Find and support cafes and restaurants that are committed to using locally sourced food and reducing waste and plastic. Apps like Fair Food Forager help to make it easier to find them in your area.

#280

Ask your local cafe to be part of the Responsible Cafe network; participating businesses offer customers a discount for bringing their own cups and containers.

#281

If you are in an unfamiliar cafe
or restaurant, have a glance around
to see what single-use plastics are being
used, such as tomato sauce (ketchup)
sachets or salad dressing in plastic cups.
Then ask for your order to have neither.

#282

If you don't think you'll use a paper
serviette when cafe staff hand you one,
give it back. Same goes for the serviette
they put under coffee cups. You can even
take a cloth one with you.

#283

Instead of using plastic coffee stirrers and cocktail mixers, opt for a reusable option, such as a spoon, or go without. Over 138 billion plastic stirrers are reportedly used and discarded worldwide each year. That's a lot of useless plastic sitting in landfill.

#284

Single-use takeaway wooden utensils, chopsticks and coffee stirrers are often heat-treated and are not always accepted by composting facilities. If you do have a home compost, place them there; otherwise provide your own or ask for a metal option.

#285

When eating out, bring along a container so you can take any leftovers home.

#286

I like to take along a cutlery wrap with utensils and a cloth napkin for eating out to avoid single-use plastic cutlery and paper napkins.

#287

Avoid the temptation of over-packaged snacks and take your own snack – fruit, cut-up vegetables, nuts and sandwiches – from home.

#288

Are you chewing plastic? Most store-bought gum contains plastic. Rest assured there are plastic-free gum brands available, like Simply Gum, which uses only natural chicle.

#289

On a warm day avoid the plastic spoon and single-use ice-cream cup: choose a waffle cone.

#290

Download the WeTap app to find public drinking fountains to refill your water bottle, instead of buying new plastic bottles.

#291

If you are travelling to a new location, consider trying to compost by using the ShareWaste app and website to help you find a public composting option like a community garden where you can leave any food scraps.

#292

Pack the picnic plates from home
on road trips or to a local festival, to avoid
takeaway in disposable containers.

#293

Avoid single-use cups by using
your reusable cup to get a cup of tea,
drink of water or glass of wine on a flight,
or at a festival or street food market.

#294

Write to restaurants and hotels with
suggestions on how they can make simple
changes to reduce their waste.

#295

Ask around to see what you can borrow from friends before buying a new esky, tent or sleeping bag for that camping trip you are planning.

#296

Ecotourism is the practice of being a responsible traveller with the mindset of leaving a minimal environmental footprint through the choices we make.

#297

The average airline passenger
creates 500 grams (1 lb 2 oz) of waste
per flight. If you do two round trips
a year, that's 2 kilograms (4 lb 6 oz)
of rubbish.

#298

Take wooden cutlery or airline-approved
cutlery to avoid the single-use plastic
on airplanes. You can make a cutlery wrap
to keep them in: otherwise upcycle a pencil case
or simply wrap them inside a tea (dish) towel
secured by a rubber band.

#299

Call ahead to check if your airline will refill your bottle while onboard as some flights don't always offer this. Your question could lead them to change their policy in the future and even ditch the single-use bottles and cups.

#300

Try to cancel your meal and take food on your next flight. Pack fresh fruit, vegetables and sandwiches in your containers that you can also use at your destination.

#301

Aim to take carry-on luggage only when flying. The heavier a plane, the more fuel is needed. Carry-on will also help avoid BPA-coated luggage stickers that can't be recycled. Don't forget to opt for e-tickets instead of the BPA paper ones too.

#302

Taking your own inflatable pillow, headphones and a large scarf onto a plane will help you avoid the plastic-wrapped pillows, headphones and blankets handed out.

#303

Hold on to small bottles to decant
your toiletries into for travelling
rather than buying new ones.

#304

Upcycle an old shower cap to use as
a shoe protector in your luggage.

#305

Rather than buy souvenirs for
everyone back home, consider
sending a postcard.

#306

On holiday, carry a long piece of string with you as a makeshift clothesline and laundry soap for handwashing garments to avoid plastic bags from your hotel's laundry service.

#307

When travelling abroad to areas where water is considered unsafe, check with local hotels if they offer refills of water or ask where the locals get their water purified. Otherwise look up portable options like the SteriPen.

#308

Local food markets are fun places to seek out and try foreign delicacies when travelling. You can also buy unpackaged food there too, while supporting small businesses and local farmers.

#309

Look up local eco-bloggers in the area you are travelling to. They are a great source of knowledge to find out what hidden eco gems are in their city or town, and they can even help you perfect how to ask for 'no straw' in their language.

#310

Try not to get discouraged if you make more waste when travelling. Tomorrow is always another day to try again.

#311

Get inquisitive and note any new eco-initiatives a town, state or country practises that you can share when you get home.

#312

Start a green team at your school
or workplace to help lead change.
You could begin by working together
to install a compost system or reduce
the amount of single-use plastic.

#313

Since we spend most of our days at work, ask if you can set up a compost, worm farm or bokashi bin in your office.

#314

Suggest a beach or river litter clean-up for your next office event. Organise it yourself or connect with a local environmental group. It's a way to teach others about reducing packaging and keeping our valuable local waterways clean.

#315

Set up a coffee mug library at your workplace to encourage colleagues to avoid single-use cups either in the office or when popping out to get a hot drink.

#316

Organise a zero-waste lunch at work by asking your co-workers to bring food that isn't packaged. It shows how reducing waste can be fun and easy.

#317

Suggest that the office purchase loose-leaf tea, refillable coffee pods, bulk sugar and refillable dishwashing liquid in bulk rather than individual tea bags, disposable coffee pods, sugar sachets and plastic-packaged dishwashing liquid.

A CONTAINER BROUGHT
FROM HOME

REUSABLE WATER
BOTTLE

#318

Try keeping a zero-waste kit at
the office for takeaway lunches. Of course,
another option is to sit in and enjoy your
meal, use cutlery already at the office
and grab a mug from the office kitchen
if you need the coffee to go.

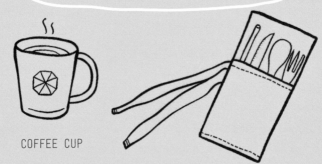

COFFEE CUP

CUTLERY IN A WRAP

#319

Consider changing your email signature to include a message about your low-waste goals and a tip on how to refuse, reduce and reuse.

#320

Audit the stationery cupboard at the office before automatically buying new stationery. You might find there are already staplers, pens and folders ready to be used.

#321

Instead of buying individual stationery, share items like sharpeners, rulers, hole punches and tape dispensers and make sure to swap to paper tape instead of plastic.

#322

Encourage double-sided printing;
this will help an office
save on money, printer ink and paper.

#323

Look for secondhand folders or
choose new ones made only of
cardboard rather than with a vinyl
covering.

#324

Used and broken pens, pencils and
markers can be recycled through
TerraCycle. Visit the website for your
country to find drop-off locations.

#325

If you need new pens at home, consider asking family and friends for any spares they have, or choose wooden pencils. There are also refillable options for pens, pacers, highlighters, whiteboard markers and plastic-free highlighters that look like pencils.

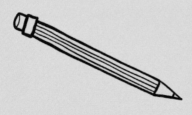

#326

Share with friends in your office
how to line a bin with old newspapers
instead of plastic bags.

#327

Swap staples for paperclips and use
scrap paper with paperclips
for sticky notes at home and the office.
Paperclips can be reused over and over again.

#328

With phone directories now available
online, call the provider to stop the annual
delivery to your home and office.

BEYOND

#329

If you are setting up a new office,
opt for secondhand desks and chairs
or hire from office furniture companies.

#330

Remove the bin from under your
office desk to help you rethink
what it is you're throwing away.

#331

If your office is saving money
from reducing waste, consider
donating that money to community
projects in need of funding.

#332

The word *activism*, usually
associated with large rallies, can be
polarising to people. But activism can
be making art or craft, writing letters,
sending packaging back, sharing a photo on
social media, signing a petition, wearing
a t-shirt or repairing things. Activism
is simply you acting on your vision
for the world.

#333

Start a book club with your
friends with environmental
sustainability as the theme. Borrow
your books from a library – or
instead of all reading the same book
each month, read different books on
the same theme (and swap ones you
like between each other).

#334

Biodegradable plastics and bioplastics promote the 'buy, use once, throw away' mentality that we need to break up with. Avoid where you can and choose reusable options.

#335

If you see litter, pick it up. It might not be yours, but the action not only helps stop plastic and other materials from polluting and causing harm to our environment, you'll also be a role model to others.

#336

Next time you are out for a run,
try *plogging*: picking up rubbish
while jogging.

#337

While individual actions matter,
the fastest way to propel change
is through legislation. Set up a meeting
with your local, state or federal
representative to discuss issues and
solutions to waste and plastic pollution.

#338

Join or start up a campaign to
stop the free distribution of plastic
bags in your town, state or country.
There have been many successful
campaigns around the world from which
you can get information and inspiration.

#339

Collectively we have the power to
dictate how goods are packaged and
presented to us, what they are made of,
where they come from and the
conditions they are made under.

#340

A handwritten letter to a business and its board of directors is a powerful way to voice your views and suggestions.
A personalised letter doesn't need to be long or angry; keep it short, state the facts and share your ideas on how the business could improve its practices.
Supply a reply address.

#341

Beware greenwashing! This is when companies claim their products are good for the environment by using words like 'eco', 'green' and 'natural' to describe them because they know customers want to make better choices. It's always good to double-check that the company walks the talk.

#342

It's not the consumers' sole responsibility to figure out if packaging can be recycled. Instead send ridiculous packaging back to the business, letting them know how they could change and why it's also their responsibility. We are not just consumers; we're citizens too.

#343

Share your story and skills on how you reduced your waste with your community. Your journey just might have the potential to inspire someone to use less packaging or start a compost.

#344

The internet has allowed us to connect and share our voices, so make use of the technology to sign and share online petitions or create a campaign with a hashtag like #nofoodwastemelbourne.

#345

Photojournalist James Wakibia created a campaign asking for a ban on plastic bags. He photographed everyday Kenyans with the hashtag #IsupportbanplasticsKE and encouraged others to use the hashtag too. Kenya banned plastic bags for household and commercial packaging in 2017.

#346

There is a growing number of community groups, like Boomerang Bags, that sew and give out cloth bags at local stores. Visit their website to join one in your area or start your own.

#347

Use art (artivism), craft (craftivism) or music to highlight plastic pollution and the solutions.

#348

Check with your local council to see if there is an environmental advisory board or committee you can join to help guide change in your community.

#349

There are more and more websites
and apps where you can shop online
for secondhand goods: eBay, Gumtree,
Craigslist, Facebook Marketplace and
a number of independent websites.

#350

Set up a Facebook group in your town or type in 'zero waste' and your area to see if one already exists. You'll be able to use the space to share local businesses that support a low-waste lifestyle and tips for living with less plastic, and connect with others in the community.

#351

Join and offer your help to a political party that is aligned with your views. You might even become inspired to run one day.

#352

Set up an information stall at
a local market, sharing the simple
swaps people can make to reduce
their waste. Bring along some
of your own cleaning and beauty
products to show people what they
can do in their own home.

#353

Hire out a local theatre, community
hall or library to host a movie night.
Eco-documentaries are a great way to share
a message. Encourage guests to bring along
unpackaged foods from home and have a
discussion after the movie. *The Clean Bin
Project, A Plastic Ocean* and *Bag It*
are popular.

#354

Put a 'No Advertising, Please' notice on your letterbox telling the delivery people you don't want a wad of junk-mail advertisements. Sure, they can be recycled, but it's still a waste of paper in the first place.

#355

Cut back on what is sent to your post box by removing yourself from mailing lists and choosing to have bills sent by email instead.

#356

Each item that comes into our lives has a narrative that often begins far away and involves people, animals, water and finite resources. Choose to support companies that care about the welfare of each.

#357

Pause and think about where your money is going. Our dollars are a vote that will shape the world for the next generation.

#358

Choosing locally made items not only cuts back on the fuel emissions needed for transportation, it also creates local jobs and improves skills and knowledge. Plus, we can more easily find out if the people making our stuff are treated fairly.

#359

Link your values with your money by swapping your bank and superannuation fund to institutions that prioritise ethical investments with the protection of the environment in mind.

#360

Enjoy the new skills you are
learning and consider sharing
them within your community.

#361

Connecting with others who are also
working towards reducing their waste,
either online or offline, is a great
way to stay motivated and
share tips too.

#362

Make time to get out into nature
with family and friends, to remember
what it is you are trying to protect
for the next generation.

#363

Don't forget to celebrate the changes you have made to reduce your waste at home and beyond. You are inspiring more people than you know.

#364

Be proud of what you have achieved! It's a collective effort and your efforts are important.

#365

There are more than 365 ways to reduce our waste. Use the lines here to record the areas you're still working towards, tips you've learnt or questions you'd like answered.

ABOUT THIS BOOK

All efforts were taken to make this book a low-waste project.
The editorial and design process was done almost entirely
on-screen, and advanced reading copies were offered
only electronically. The entire book is printed on Forest
Stewardship Council (FSC) certified stock. FSC is the highest
standard forest certification scheme and the only one to
be a member of ISEAL Alliance, the global association for
sustainability standards. The paper is cut to size prior to
printing in order to reduce wastage. The printing itself is in
soy-based inks, which are more sustainable and produce less
volatile organic compounds (VOCs) than their petroleum-
based alternatives and makes it easier for the paper to
eventually be recycled. All excess paper, plastic, wood and
metal (such as printing plates) produced during the printing
process will be recycled, as will any extra inventory (hopefully
there isn't any!).

ABOUT THE AUTHOR

Erin Rhoads has been writing about her zero-waste journey since 2013. Her blog, The Rogue Ginger, quickly became one of Australia's most popular eco-lifestyle websites, and Erin is now a prominent commentator on zero-waste living. She divides her time consulting with businesses on waste reduction, sharing skills and ideas at workshops and talks for kids and adults around Australia, and participating in environmental action groups.

Erin was a consultant on Australia's *War on Waste* and is a regular contributor on ABC Radio. She has been featured on BBC World, *The Project, Sunrise, The Age, The Guardian, The Australian Women's Weekly, Marie Claire, Peppermint* magazine and many more.

Erin lives in Melbourne, Australia, with her husband and son. *Waste Not Everyday* is her second book.

Published in 2019 by Hardie Grant Books,
an imprint of Hardie Grant Publishing

Hardie Grant Books (Melbourne)
Building 1, 658 Church Street
Richmond, Victoria 3121

Hardie Grant Books (London)
5th & 6th Floors
52–54 Southwark Street
London SE1 1UN

hardiegrantbooks.com

A catalogue record for this
book is available from the
National Library of Australia

Waste Not Everyday
ISBN 978 1 74379 555 2

10 9 8 7 6 5 4 3

Publisher: Arwen Summers
Project Editor: Joanna Wong
Editor: Susan Keogh
Design Manager: Jessica Lowe
Design and illustrations: Grace West
Production Manager: Todd Rechner

Colour reproduction by Splitting Image Colour Studio
Printed by Leo Paper Products LTD.

The paper this book is printed on is from FSC®-certified
forests and other sources. FSC® promotes environmentally
responsible, socially beneficial and economically viable
management of the world's forests.